C000027545

AROUND
DROITWICH
IN OLD PHOTOGRAPHS

Brine Bath.
Park.
GWR
COPYRIGHT
R.T. & S. LTD

Impney Park.
G.W.R.

Droitwich.
DTH. 66.

Terrace Gardens Impney Hotel.
GWR

Worcestershire Hotel Grounds.
GWR

AROUND
DROITWICH
IN OLD PHOTOGRAPHS

COLLECTED BY
JOHN BRETTELL

ALAN SUTTON
1989

Alan Sutton Publishing
Gloucester

First published 1989

British Library Cataloguing in Publication Data

Around Droitwich in old photographs.
1. Hereford and Worcester. Droitwich, history
I. Brettell, J.O.
942.4′49

ISBN 0-86299-619-8

Typesetting and origination by
Alan Sutton Publishing
Printed in Great Britain by
Dotesios Printers Limited

CONTENTS

SAL SAPIT OMNIA

DROITWICH.

To my dearest wife for all her patience and understanding. 1989.

INTRODUCTION

I so enjoyed putting together my first book of old pictures of Droitwich in 1987, that, following the compliments and suggestions from contacts, it took very little persuasion for me to undertake the pleasant task of developing this second book.

We are acquiring new additions to our stock of old pictures all the time, especially if one hunts as hard as we do – whether this be from old newspapers, postcards or anything else photographical with the aid of modern techniques. This, coupled with trust and help from interested people who will lend, sell or even give their precious items, makes it all that much easier. In the process of collecting for this book, I found that there were so many superb pictures of some of the villages surrounding Droitwich, that I could not on any account leave them out. So the idea was born to present a collection of old pictures of Droitwich with help from some of the local villages. This you will see as you turn the pages of this little book, and marvel at the happenings and happiness of years gone by.

However, the heart of this book is Droitwich Spa, as I like to call it. You will see that this time, while buildings and town are included, the main theme is people and personalities. The first book (sorry but I do have to compare), was aimed at the newer residents of Droitwich to show them, and refresh the memory of others, how our town looked years ago. This book also does that, but brings in more of the human element.

'Salinae', or Droitwich as we call it today, has had its lifestyle formed on salt, from the Romans and Saxons through until today, where the brine is used at the new Brine Baths. If you visit the Heritage Centre, brightly coloured brochures will tell you how all this came about; how the brine is pumped from underground, it's density, how it is used and all the necessary information to make you wonder at the marvels of nature. One very important point to make here is that few people realise the difference in our spa town from most of the others: we bathe in our water, they drink theirs.

Droitwich is blessed with some superb hotels, all built and developed within the last century by John Corbett, the so-called Salt King of Droitwich. From the dazzling Impney, (renamed the Chateau Impney by the late Ralph Edwards), the Raven Hotel and the at present closed Worcestershire Hotel to the other small hotels and guest houses, accommodation was offered to the patients who came to be cured of their afflictions. It should be noted here that the Impney did not become a hotel until sometime after John Corbett's death.

Droitwich is now suffering from the effects of modernization. We seem to have got used to the precinct and the benefits (?) that it brings to the town, and now the next step, the pedestrianization of the High Street is being thrust upon us. One can only hope that some of old Droitwich will be left; even if it is only an old shop front with a modern back, that will be better than nothing.

Savour and enjoy the village pictures – they are such a joy to look at; the cornfield, the pubs, the traction engines and so many other lovely sights, they make one wonder what it is that we have left.

My wife and I have enjoyed searching for these pictures over the last two years, and have even widened our circle of friends by it – it is hoped that you also think it was all worth while.

If all goes well, who knows, perhaps there will be another book in two or three years time, the mark three edition – it is up to you!

The best way to start a book of pictures is on a light note, so here we have some comic cards, all posted from Droitwich, to send us on our way. The heyday of the postcard was from around 1900 to 1916, when it was the done thing to send home a comic card, to tell everyone what a lovely time was being had by all. Postcards were cheap, 1d. each at the most and the postage was only ½d. – there were not many telephones in those days, so the need was there. Some of the great names of comic card artists, such as Cyncicus, GEF and McGill are included in this small selection.

Tearing ourselves away
from **Droitwich**

Having a Pick-Me-Up at
DROITWICH

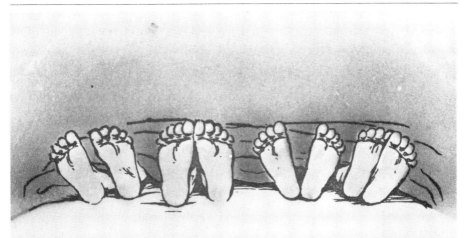

Come and rest your weary feet
at Droitwich

I AM ON A GOOD THING HERE—COME AND JOIN ME
At Droitwich

Basking in the sunshine
at Droitwich

For a quiet retreat it can't be beat!
Come and join us at
Droitwich

IN FULL SWING

AT DROITWICH

This is a 'living' village, and it is still lucky enough to retain amenities that others seem to have lost, like; its own village shop, garage, riding school, dentist and of course the pub. For many hundreds of years the land provided work for the men of the village. Some out-work was contracted to the women from the Worcester glove factories – this has now passed on, as it has in the City. The small farms have also been absorbed into the bigger ones. The main event of the year, besides the parades, May Day celebrations and other events, was the Spring steeplechase meeting held around Climbers Hill – two pictures appear later in this book – sadly this was discontinued at the outbreak of the Second World War.

LEST WE FORGET

A Patriotic Poem

By Agnes Churchill Stockley

Let us remember the Comrades we have known,
The Flower of Britain's manhood, from many a happy home,
who answered to their Country's call, to them we owe a debt,
Let us pray for unity and peace – lest we forget.

We promised to remember the men of yesterday,
the debt we owe to them is one we never can repay.
Some are gone beyond recall, but some are with us yet,
Let us lend a helping hand to them – lest we forget.

Let us pray our Heavenly Father that He will ever be,
with those who serve their Country, in the air, on land and sea.
We are subjects of an empire where the sun is never set,
let us pray for Brotherhood and peace – lest we forget.

Written at Crowle May 1944.

THIS IS CHURCH ROAD, C. 1912. Approaching with their bikes are Miss Annie Bunn and Mr Griffin, with the lovely beard, who is headmaster of the local school.

AGAIN CHURCH ROAD, but this time showing Mrs Hanna Holt with her two children Hilda and Vera taken around 1912.

TWO FINE PICTURES of the landed gentry with their 'Rollers' and carriages, drawn, no doubt, by the finest of horses, attending the Cowle Point-to-Point Steeplechases in April 1910.

THIS SUPERB PICTURE of men and horse, all helping to build a corn rick at Commandry Farm, Lower Crowle in 1910.

NO DOUBT THE 'LIKELY LADS', one Sunday afternoon in their best caps, on the green outside Chequers Farm around 1916.

THE FRONT SHELL GARDEN of Radcliffe House in 1935. It was designed and built over a number of years by Mr Alfred Marks.

THESE GOOD LADIES have just completed the organization of the Annual Strawberry Tea, which is always held in the gardens of the vicarage. Here it was in 1926.

ASSEMBLED HERE in 1926 are the members of the Crowle Tennis Club in the grounds of Bleak House.

THIS SOMBRE BUILDING is the house of Mordants Farm as it looked in 1920.

THE GREEN FARM belonged to the Froxmere estate until 1928, and contained some 112 acres.

TWO FINE PICTURES of the local football team, with the Revd John Davis, around 1920.

THE PUPILS OF CROWLE SCHOOL around 1910, with their teachers the Miss Griffin sisters, far left and far right. Look at the lad top left — he would make a good prop forward.

HERE WE HAVE CROWLE SCHOOL again, but this time in 1928, with Mr Woodhead the school master.

LOCALS AND THEIR ANIMALS pose at the Chequers Inn, Crowle around 1909. It has changed a bit since this picture was taken.

LOCAL MEN again outside the Chequers Inn, but here around 1912. What about the chap in the light (?) suit?

A PICTURE OF CROWLE CHURCH taken at Christmas time in 1902, when the Revd J. Bamber was the vicar.

THIS LOVELY WEDDING GROUP pictures the marriage of Mr Joseph Cooper and Miss Elsie Sherwood at Crowle in 1916.

The name of this village has been known in farming circles for hundreds of years, but like so many other communities, modern times have taken away the farm workers to the nearby towns, due to mechanization. The biggest drain of labour has been to nearby Kidderminster, where the carpet industry has welcomed them with open arms. The addition of 'Corbett' to the name Chaddesley was made when a rich and famous family moved to the area during Norman times. They developed and laid out the original village as we know it today, together with rebuilding the church. Now the village has become a dormitory town for the city workers, but at least they have something very special to come home to.

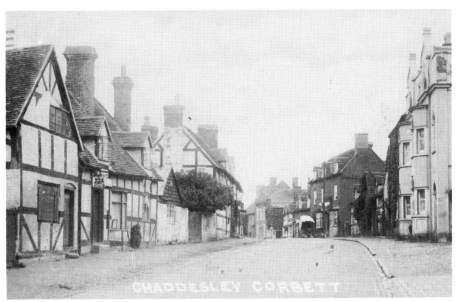

TODAY THESE BUILDINGS are very desirable residences, whereas about fifty years ago they were the homes and businesses of the local cobbler, saddler, tailor and many other country trades.

CHADDESLEY VILLAGE, Near KIDDERMINSTER.

A VILLAGE STREET of years ago, where children could play without danger from passing traffic, as shown by the carefree attitude and smiling faces.

ANOTHER VIEW taken further down the street when the children were at school, and there, in the middle a 'drop head' Ford car is just visible.

A VERY BUSY SCENE when the Albrighton Woodland Hunt meet with the hounds on Bank Holiday Monday in 1910.

THE INTERIOR OF ST CASSIAN'S CHURCH, rebuilt by the Corbett family in the fourteenth century, and the focal point of village life.

ANOTHER FOCAL POINT for some people, the Talbot, where weary travellers can quench their thirst and ease their hunger. It comes highly recommended!

The village, somehow escaping the developer's eye, is now more of a dormitory town than a place of industry. Many years ago some work was done in favour of the needle influence from Redditch, but that has now passed by. In the centre of the village is the lovely old Church of St John the Baptist, the doors of which are sadly locked in the week to keep out, one assumes, the undesirable element of our modern society, to the detriment of genuine church lovers. The old chestnut tree near the tower is a shadow of its former self, due to gales, which broke the straps holding it together. Buried here, in a grave surrounded by railings, is the queen of the gipsies, Phoebe Lee, who died over a hundred years ago. With the busy main road cutting through the village it still maintains an air of dignity and peace and quiet, no doubt encouraged by the stream that meanders through the west side.

OVER THE NARROW BRIDGE towards Droitwich. Little has changed along this road over many years.

High Street, Feckenham

TWO PICTURES showing both sides of Main Street taken at around the turn of the century. The two shops pictured look as if there is a bit of competition between them, as they both were hardware stores. However, the left hand one has the edge on the other as it is also the post office.

THE CHURCH OF ST JOHN THE BAPTIST is situated at the top of a long path right in the heart of Feckenham.

THE VICAR, here in the early nineteen hundreds, had not only a lovely church, but also a very grand vicarage.

A TYPICAL VICTORIAN SCHOOL, but how well the pupils seem to be dressed in their knee-breeches and caps.

I WONDER IF THIS SPOT, with the man on the bridge, is still so quiet and peaceful today as it was then?

Again, a small living community spread over quite a large area, hemmed in on either side by the steep, red sandstone rock and bounded on three sides by water. On this cultivated and fertile land grows many an oak tree in the well-known Shrawley Woods, now partly managed by the Forestry Commission. It is justly proud of its very old Church of St Mary, which, with gentle repairs, has withstood the passage of time. However, in the last few years a lot of money had to be raised to carry out some major projects to make it safe for use – this was successfully accomplished. Shrawley lies on the Worcester to Stourport road, and if you have the time, and wish to avoid the rush of the modern day traffic, this should be your route.

A SUPER 'ACTION' PHOTOGRAPH of the cider makers at Wood Farm around 1908.

THE RECTORY. The home at this moment in time of the Revd H.T. Boultbee and his family.

THE SCHOOL AND SCHOOL HOUSE known to many of the older members of the community. With all the changes in education it now serves as the village hall.

THESE TWO PICTURES show the two school classes all washed and scrubbed for the photographer, taken around 1905.

THE ANCIENT ORDER OF FORESTERS prior to their club walk, again around 1910.

SHRAWLEY SCHOOL CONCERT 1923 under the eye of the two teachers, Mr & Mrs Thomas. Amongst the girls are Phyllis & Muriel Medlicott, Joan and Nancy Crane, Vernal & Gladys Verity, May & Olive Dounes, Mary Oakley, Edith Compton and Elsie Wilcox.

ANOTHER GROUP of the Ancient Order of Foresters prior to their summer ramble. What a lovely car and, oh, the hats!

A CROWD OF YOUNGSTERS admire the camera at Hexton's Corner, – the corner you meet as you come into the village.

THE KNOWLE. A thatched roofed cottage as lovely now as it was then. It was the home of Miss Annie Rowley.

THIS GRAND LITTLE COTTAGE served the people of Shrawley as the post office for many years.

THE FETE COMMITTEE for 1924. Standing Messrs: Munslow, Brookes, Vernon, Clark, Weaver, Colwill, Bunce, Averill, Lucas and White. Seated, Mesdames: Everett, Allen, Vernon, Thomas and Mr Baldwin. On the grass Messrs: Gittens, Hodgkinson, Thomas, Spragg, Boultbee and Turford.

THE CHURCH CHOIR of 1925 with such names as Rowley, Watkins, Westwood, Jones, Walker, Oakey, Powick, Anderson, Farmer, Parsons, Jones, Crane, Weaver, Hodgkinson, Hall, Turford and Smith.

THE ROSE & CROWN, now under the watchful eye of Mr Jim Hoskins. It is well-known for its cool beer and good food.

THE NEW INN, another of the well liked places in the village. Note the bikes and no cars – forsight no doubt, regarding the breath test!

A HAPPY PICTURE of Mr & Mrs Charles Lea standing outside their home, Caldcotts, in 1934.

THE ROSE AND CROWN FOOTBALL TEAM in 1909 on their way to a match.

THE WOMEN'S INSTITUTE basket making class, taken outside their headquarters in 1911. The only man being the instructor Mr J. Large.

THE GIRLS' FRIENDLY SOCIETY. Who can you recognise in this group: ? Jones, Nelly Jauncey, Majorie Lucas, Nelly Pratley, ? Poultney, Kathleen Lake, Peggy Jones, Louise Bullock, Nora Lucas, Mary Pilkington, Anne Rowley, Gladys Cliff, Mabel Farmer, Nelly Anderson & Ethel Hall?

The village is divided by the A38 between Droitwich and Bromsgrove, just north of the M5 junction. It is surrounded by villages smaller than itself on which it exerts some influence, excepting probably Stoke Prior. Here John Corbett had his great salt works, transforming the conditions for his working people; giving them better housing, and best of all, continuous employment. His generosity also provided for the building of a school, a church, a vicarage and even almshouses for his retired employees. The locally well-known Amphlett family lived at Wychbold Hall. The first hall was demolished because of subsidence, then in 1937 a new hall was built, and remained in the family until 1955. In the centre of the village is the Crown Inn, dating back to the early seventeen hundreds. It has been modernized more than once, and even today is due to close for further 'refurbishment'.

WYCHBOLD can be spotted from miles around, due to the twin masts at the BBC. They were built between 1932 and 1934 and the station began broadcasting in April of 1934 with the, what was in those days well-known, 'Droitwich Calling'. However, I understand that in the next year or so, these masts are going to be demolished, having outlived their usefulness. Another casualty of modern times and techniques.

TODAY you could never see a sight like this – the A38 in the early 1920s, but I suppose we all get used to the age and pace in which we are brought up.

WIRELESS STATION, DROITWICH.

THE MAIN BUILDING OF BBC WYCHBOLD which was built in the early 1920s, to replace another wireless station at a cost of about a quarter of a million pounds. Nothing to what it would cost today.

A GATHERING OF LOCAL PARISHIONERS to make a presentation of £50 to the Revd. R. Male towards the cost of a stained glass window. Taken on 31 August 1909.

The Revd R. Male planting two silver birch trees, also on 31 August 1909, on the twenty-first anniversary of the consecration of St Mary De Wyche Church.

ANOTHER LOVELY PICTURE of the celebrations to mark the anniversary of the consecration of the church.

ANOTHER OF JOHN CORBETT'S GIFTS to the area – the almshouses nestling below the masts, where the elderly are well looked after by a resident caretaker. Officially known as the Corbett Cottage Homes.

This lovely small village is situated to the north of Droitwich, on the B road to Kidderminster and Stourport. Like so many other villages of today, it has become a dormitory site, a lot of small farms have been eaten up by their larger bretheren, the local trades have disappeared and there is not even a bus service. All the photographs except the picture of the postman in this section, are about the local school, and feature a teacher named 'Florrie'. Would that you could read the backs of these picture postcards by this 'Florrie', who seems to have been a prolific letter or card writer to a friend 'Susan'. However, she tucked each card into an envelope for safer delivery I suppose, so we shall never find out who this mysterious Susan is, or where she lived, as the envelopes did not survive. You will see how the story unfolds as you read the captions below the pictures.

A GROUP OF CHILDREN outside the local school, however, no writing on the back of this card, just a series of question marks. I understand that this picture was taken around 1908.

WILLIAM HENRY PRIDDEY with his granddaughter Ethel, wearing with pride his postman's uniform showing his Long Service Medal and Certificate of service from the Post Office. He was born in 1845 and was postman from 1871 until his retirement in 1905, he died in 1929.

FLORRIE WRITES , 'this is a picture of us with the boss – he has just told us a HMI is coming next week – do I look frightened?'

NAMED HERE are some of the pupils above: Nell Brown, Bertha Bugley, Bertie Padget, Mollie Williamson, Archie Morris, Marian Clinton, Elsie Lunnon, May Middleton, Francis Farmer, May Farmer, Jane Knight, Alice Knight and the one with the cross on her tummy is Ethel Priddey, c. 1908.

AGAIN FLORRIE WRITES, 'do you like my new skirt and what do you think of me now?' The only other clue is that she was staying at a place called 'Norchard' Stourport. . .?

A small village without a pub. However, it has many self-generated interests to compensate for this. It stands a few miles south of Droitwich between the River Salwarpe and the Droitwich canal. The home of a lovely fourteenth-century church, St Michael and all Angels, and the inspiring site of Salwarpe court, about which many stories have been written. Now, as is the fashion, some of its barns have been converted to modern homes, thus bringing new blood into the parish to keep its reputation for being a warm and friendly place. The canal which used to be alive with boats hauling salt from Droitwich, soon went into disuse and decay when this ceased, but now the Droitwich Canal Trust have opened it up, and you can now take a cruise down its length in a gaily coloured barge, walk along the tow-path, fish or do whatever takes your fancy.

Salwarpe Canal and Bridge.

Salwarpe Canal.

DROITWICH

TWO SIMPLE BUT REVEALING PICTURES of the canal at Salwarpe, showing all the beauty of the trees and surroundings.

DROITWICH. THE CANAL AT SALWARPE.

SALWARPE COURT, a house with its own built-in history; from Catherine of Aragon, to the Yorkists, right through the ages until today. It is now being carefully restored.

INCREASE from 4 CWT. OF KAINIT, | WHEAT, 7½ BUSHELS.
| STRAW, 6¼ CWT.

AN ADVERTISEMENT CARD showing the results after the use of 'Kainit' fertiliser on a crop of wheat at Walnut Tree Farm. Postally used in September 1905.

S 9798 Salwarpe Church, Droitwich

THE FOURTEENTH-CENTURY CHURCH of St Michael and all Angels. Above is shown the lychgate and below, the interior. Now under the care of the Revd John Willis.

This is a large sprawling parish with the roots of history firmly planted in its very fertile soil. The village is blessed with a huge oak tree in the centre by the roundabout, a sight not to be missed in the autumn with all its colour. Nearby is the beautiful Church of St Andrews, and of course the Manor of Ombersley, the home of the Sandys family since 1560. There is a wealth of half-timbered houses and so much history is written into them, that it is a subject on its own. I have taken the liberty of including Hadley with Ombersley, as they are so close together, and while not dependent on each other, one can say that Hadley looks to Ombersley to lead the way.

THE MOST POPULAR WAY to say 'hello, having a lovely holiday' – the postcard that shows lots of views of the village.

THE ROAD FROM KIDDERMINSTER up to what is now an island, and showing the local post office with a young customer.

OVER THE ISLAND to the Crown & Sandys Hotel in the distance, avoiding the chap in the road in the smart breeches, however!

Ombersley Village.

ANOTHER VIEW, this time heading north with the Crown & Sandys on your right, and the Kings Arms at top right. Two for the price of one.

Ombersley, near Worcester

A NEAR 'FULL FRONTAL' of the Kings Arms, with the children playing in the street. Today, it is so popular that you virtually have to queue to get a drink and a snack.

THESE LOVELY COTTAGES are in Sinton Lane and are well worth a visit, to see what half-timbered cottages should be like.

ON THE CORNER of the main road and Sinton Lane, this forge with the horseshoe entrance still stands. Alas, no longer used for the purpose for which it was designed, but still used as a forge for making iron gates and, in fact, anything to order.

ST ANDREW'S CHURCH which has watched over the people of Ombersley for over 150 years. In 1828 it replaced the old St Ambrose's Church.

THE POST OFFICE again with the familiar sight of a horse and cart, taken, judging by the shadow, at midday.

OMBERSLEY INSTITUTE Air Gun Club. A picture taken showing off all the trophies around October of 1910.

LORD SANDYS' SHOOTING PARTY at Ombersley Court 'ready for the off', with the beaters below, all dressed for the part in look-alike clothes, and not forgetting the jar of cider. November 1910.

Hadley Cross,   Near Ombersley.

THE CROSS HOUSE at Hadley Cross, still looking today as if it should be the home of the lord of the manor.

A QUIET ROAD with the Cross House in the background. Travelling by horse and cart is not the thing to do today with all the traffic about.

I have taken the liberty of joining Great Witley with Little Witley together under the same heading; after all, the Earl of Dudley is still Lord of the Witleys. Great Witley is the big sister and embraces the remains of the once fabulous Witley Court, with its splendid Baroque church. The growth of Witley Court year by year, owner by owner, is a story to tell all on its own. From small beginnings it grew to become a byword for luxury and elegance. The few pictures in this book will in no way reflect the absolute majesty and beauty of the court as it used to be. Then of course, there is the Hundred House, with a chequered but interesting existance from the eighteenth century up until today, where the best of food and wine are offered to an appreciative public. Little Witley is a quiet and tranquil village with around 200 inhabitants set in a very fertile belt of land, below Woodbury and Abberley Hills.

LOOKING THROUGH THE POSEIDON FOUNTAIN towards the magnificent Witley Court. This must have been a wonderful sight.

A MONTAGE OF PICTURES on a card for posting from Little Witley, showing some of its main features.

ROUND HOUSE. GREAT WITLEY.

THE ROUND HOUSE which in its 'youth', used to be a toll-house at the junction of the roads to Abberley and Bromyard.

FOUNTAIN AT WITLEY COURT

THE FOUNTAIN weighs over twenty tons and depicts Perseus saving Andromeda from the monster sent by Poseidon.

GREAT WITLEY CHAPEL.

THIS CHAPEL AND BURIAL GROUND were given to the people of Great Witley by Lord Dudley. It is now used as a headquarters for the Scouts and Guides and services have been transferred to the Baroque church at the Court.

THIS LITTLE CHURCH of St Michael and all Angels is tucked away up Church Lane. The present church dates back to the late eighteen hundreds. It is now under the Benefice of Shrawley, the Witleys and Astley.

THIS MAGNIFICENT PULPIT, is a later addition, which catches the eye as you enter the Baroque church. The iron balustrade was incorporated into the design by William Forsyth.

THE MEET at the Hundred House, Great Witley, is always something to look forward to for young and old.

THE HOME OF VARIOUS VICARS of the Witleys has been made here for many years.

THE HUNDRED HOUSE at Great Witley which dates back many years, and has been the setting for stock sales, court room and cells for some sessions, having had its origin in the eighteenth century.

ANOTHER VIEW of the Hundred House which today has been tastefully modernized to attend to the wants and whims of the public, which it succeeds in doing.

THIS SMALL SCHOOL at Little Witley has for many years been the place where the local boys and girls have had their first taste of education, and by the dating, also the cane.

A LIVING TRIBUTE to the green fingers of the local population, their ever popular Horticultural Show, a main feature on the village calendar.

This is a small village in a cluster of villages, dominated by Hanbury and Crowle. However, while it has lost most of its amenities, such as the local policeman, post office and shop, it is a happy community and nestles around its pub, the Galton Arms, the manor and the church, this dating back to the tenth century. Bow Brook, which runs through the village is prone to flooding after heavy rain, but it is accepted as part of the life that is Himbleton. However, for all its faults on paper, it is loved and cherished by the people who live there, and by those who would like to live there as well.

SOME OF THE GUESTS attending Himbleton Garden Fête at the Manor in 1912. In the background is the vicar who was ever present at functions like this.

TWO PICTURES of Himbleton Church, taken at the turn of the century, before electricity had been installed.

ONE OF THE JUNIOR CLASSES at Himbleton School taken in 1937.

AN EARLIER PICTURE of Himbleton School pupils all dressed up for the Christmas concert in 1926.

A STEAM ROLLER belonging to Droitwich Rural District Council with Mr William Tyler of Himbleton, who is standing third from the right.

A GROUP OF CHILDREN at the local school being 'drilled' with staves, by a gentleman who delights in the name of Sergeant Knight, in 1903.

AN UNCOMMON SIGHT today, a gang of hop pickers at Court Farm Himbleton in 1912.

THE SUNDAY SCHOOL TEA PARTY held at Himbleton Manor by the kind invitation of Lady Galton, around 1910. Look at all those lovely hats.

A hamlet six miles east of Worcester, five miles south of Droitwich and within the parishes of Crowle, Himbleton and Oddingley. Being situated on high ground, before there were mains water connections, the population had to rely on one well, which in dry weather had a nasty habit of drying up, and water rationing was the order of the day. Dare I mention that the two pubs, the Fox Inn and the Holly Bush are now closed. However, it is not far to the next village to obtain liquid refreshment.

The work of the local people varied from wood cutting in Trench, Sale Green and Sillet Woods, to farming, fruit growing and some hop picking. Altogether a small but happy community, so I am told.

A GROUP OF TREE FELLERS (lumberjacks?) at Sale Green around 1900. Note the old man in the front guarding the stone jar of scrumpy or the like.

AN 'INVACH' steam roller, operated by Bomford and Evershed, Salford Prior, near Evesham, and driven by Mr William Wells of Sale Green.

THE HOLLY BUSH INN with some of the regulars and the licensee, Mr George Perkins, posing for the camera around 1912.

ANOTHER GROUP OF THIRSTY WORKERS with the inevitable dogs outside the Holly Bush Inn, c. 1910.

The records of the village go back to the time of the Domesday Book, when it belonged to the church in Worcester. It is a large parish with the centre of the village being dominated by the pub, the well-known Vernon Arms. It was named after the Vernon family who came into the area in 1631. They acquired the land and built the beautiful Hanbury Hall, which is now in the care of the National Trust and welcomes visitors nearly all the year round. The Bearcrofts of Mere Hall, landowners and gentry, were also a great influence on village life and entertained many of the local people and children. Hanbury was once well-known for its stock sales, which were held regularly in spring and autumn at the Vernon Arms and in a field where the garage now stands.

S.W. VIEW, HANBURY HALL, N? DROITWICH. 4.

A QUICK GLIMPSE of Hanbury Hall as it looked some thirty years ago. It was built on land purchased in 1631 by Edward Vernon and completed in 1701. The family were involved with Hanbury over many generations.

HANBURY BAZAAR was held at Hanbury Hall on 2 August 1911. This small crowd watches the afternoon's events.

A STATELY LOOKING GENTLEMAN and girls in white dresses and black stockings listen intently to a speaker at the bazaar.

LADY VERNON makes her speech of welcome, accompanied by the vicar, to start things going at the bazaar.

BEFORE THE GAMES AND RACES commence Lady Vernon presents the Rose Bowl for the Horticultural Society.

THE CHILDREN PLAY around the maypole with my friend the vicar keeping an eye on things.

HANBURY CHURCH, built in the twelfth century, is situated on the outskirts of the village, and still attracts a large congregation when services are held there.

A ROW OF COTTAGES in two pictures, taken at the same time on the Bromsgrove Road. The group of children in the top left-hand corner seem to have nipped down to the bottom picture to help the photographer inject some life into his work. In the background is the well-known Vernon Arms which is still there today.

TWO PICTURES of a well-known garage and the family that have run it for many years, the Rudges. In the lower picture we can see Henry Charles Rudge on the right and at his side, his brother Cecil.

Here I have joined Holt, or Holt Castle as it was known, to Holt Heath, to give a broader picture of life as it used to be in the 'good old days'. Although the village has moved away from Holt Castle and St Martin's church to straddle the road, not a lot has changed. Fishing is, and always has been, a popular pastime on the nearby River Severn, whether with rod and line, or as it used to be, by netting. The two local hotels, the Fleet and the Wharf, together with the Red Lion Inn, offer a warm welcome to all that come to their doors. At Holt Mill, the YMCA has for many years organized the holiday of a lifetime for thankful children. Many acres of fertile land have in the last few years, been scarred by opencast sand and gravel digging, but as each section is finished, so it is landscaped back to its former glory.

River Severn from Holt Fleet   I feel in perfect harmony with my
                                                      surroundings here

THIS PICTURE SAYS IT ALL. The peace and quiet of the countryside, looking down the river towards the bridge.

Holt Fleet Bridge.

THESE TWO PICTURES show the bridge, designed by Telford and opened in 1838, together with a family out for a walk. Note the steamers in the background. Taken in the early 1900s.

HOLT FLEET BRIDGE

THE FLEET HOTEL as it used to be, a rendezvous for the steamers from Worcester and Stourport. Now of course, it has been completely modernized and is a great attraction for motorists as well as the lovers of the river.

HOLT FLEET had a reputation at one time for salmon catching, and some are still caught there today. This picture shows the use of nets and straw funnels – not very sportsman like.

HOLT MILL, which you could easily pass by if you were unaware of where to turn off. It was kept very spick and span by the late Mr Gardner.

THE MILL is here in the background. With the sound of rushing waters and tea laid in the garden, what more could you wish for on a summer's afternoon.

THE MILL HOUSE was used for a time as a base for the Youth Hostel Association, still under the care of Mr Gardner.

THE WELL-KNOWN LOCAL, the Red Lion, situated at the crossroads. At this time there was no garage and the road was somewhat quieter.

ST MARTIN'S CHURCH, which dates back many hundreds of years, is adjacent to Holt Castle, the home in the past of many titled families.

A FAMILY GATHERING to watch the men sheep-shearing in June of 1910. The men are still wearing their hats and waistcoats for this skilful job. It must have been hot.

With this selection of pictures of Droitwich from the late nineteenth century onwards, some idea can be gleaned as to what life was like in days gone by. The Saline Baths, the Royal Hotel and George Inn of the 1830s, the Chateau Impney of our day, intermingle these with floods, death, politicians, traditions, religions, hospitals and, of course salt, and you have our own Droitwich, or is it Wychavon's?

The main attraction of Droitwich was, and now once again is, the Brine Baths opened in 1985. Here, brine ten times stronger than sea water, containing two and a half lbs of salt per gallon, is pumped in a diluted state into a pool for the benefit of a health conscious general public.

CHATEAU IMPNEY

DROITWICH

THE BEAUTIFUL CHATEAU IMPNEY. Renamed thus by Mr Ralph Edwards, who took the old and run-down Impney, and turned it into one of the finest hotels in the Midlands.

A VIEW FROM THE LOUNGE at the Chateau Impney showing the sweeping lawns, statues, fountain and the trees that hide Droitwich.

THE GROTTO at the Chateau where in the humid temperature exotic plants and fruit were once grown. It has now been demolished.

WORKMEN at the Chateau in 1951 extending the ballroom amidst a web of scaffolding. This was a difficult job as the walls were up to two feet wide.

THE PARK HOTEL as it was called at the turn of the century, in the hands of John Corbett. It was then passed on to the Platts family, and finally became The Heriots, a home for the elderly.

THE NEW LOUNGE at the Park Hotel. It was right up to date, including indoor palms and uncomfortable looking whicker chairs.

THE RAVEN HOTEL which at a quick glance looks almost as it is today. This was another Corbett enterprise, developing it from a manor house into a luxurious hotel in 1887.

THE MAIN ENTRANCE HALL of the Raven Hotel before a dividing wall was erected and most of it became a well-frequented lounge bar.

THE COFFEE ROOM of the Royal Hotel which was situated at the corner of Queen Street and Hanbury Street.

TAKEN IN AROUND 1905, this picture looks down St Andrews Street with the Raven Hotel on the right.

A GRAND PICTURE of the Raven Hotel together with the old Salters Hall, taken in the early 1900s.

A SIDE VIEW of the Raven Hotel and Salters Hall, which tells us on the notice board that a film called *The Main Event* is now showing.

12/7 Salters Hall, Droitwich

THE OLD SALTERS HALL photographed in 1910. An old charabanc is trying to tempt people into going out for a run in the country.

A LINE OF BATH CHAIRS on one side, and a taxi and bus on the other, outside the Salters Hall.

AYRSHIRE HOUSE, advertised first as a private boarding establishment, it then became an office block and is at present a home for the elderly.

Ayrshire House and Corbett Avenue, Droitwich Spa

ANOTHER VIEW of Ayrshire House situated at the junction of Lyttelton Road and Corbett Avenue.

THE IMPOSING WORCESTERSHIRE BRINE BATHS HOTEL built by John Corbett in 1891 from two half-finished houses at a cost of £20,000.

THE NEW LOUNGE at the Worcestershire, as it was known locally, where no expense was spared to obtain unashamed luxury.

THE ST ANDREW'S HOUSE HOTEL is a small privately run hotel, but what it lacks in size it makes up for with warmth and hospitality.

THE NORBURY HOUSE HOTEL completed before the First World War, and described in such glowing terms as, 'an extremely well administered country house.'

THE BALLROOM at the Norbury where I understand lavish balls were held, together with tea dances on Saturdays.

THE KITCHENS where 'the food is English and excellent and is prepared with such care and thought', as it said in the book advertising the hotel.

THE ABOVE BOOK also says of the bedrooms, 'the draws in your dressing table do not stick, nor do the wardrobes squeak'.

THE SALINE BATHS and Hotel from a steel engraving as it looked in 1867.

THE ROYAL HOTEL AND GEORGE INN erected on the east side of Queen Street at its junction with Hanbury Street in 1836. It was demolished in 1900.

FOR PATIENTS OF LIMITED MEANS, the Royal Brine Baths Clinic could offer full board, medical supervision, brine baths and massage, all for three and a half guineas per week.

THE SUN RAYS HOTEL offered comfort and help for patients attending the clinics. It is now a retirement home.

THE BRINE BATHS on the right with the Winter Gardens on the left. It was said that you could be cured of your infirmaties on the one side, and prove it on the dance floor on the other.

INSIDE THE WINTER GARDENS having a cup of tea. Tea dances and other functions were held here regularly.

THE OLD COCK INN , Friar Street, licensed since 1712 in the reign of Queen Anne. The ecclesiastical window came from the nearby St Nicholas' Church which was destroyed in the seventeenth century.

A CLOSER LOOK at the hideous stone masks on the front of the pub. One is said to be like the infamous hanging judge, Judge Jefferies.

ALBERT EDWARDS, father of the late Ralph Edwards, last owner of the Royal Exchange, Queen Street. It was sold to Flowers Brewery in around 1922.

ANOTHER VIEW of the Exchange, as it was known, showing Queen Street running up to Chapel Bridge.

ST GEORGES SQUARE during the 1924 flood that also flooded the High Street very badly.

A LOVELY WOODED HILL? No, this is the Witton Hill or the A38 as it is called today.

High Street, Droitwich

THE TOP AND THE BOTTOM, or the east and the west of High Street, which is still the main thoroughfare despite all the other attempts to shift the interest to the 'concrete square'.

Have you tried the "PERFECT LOAF?" If not, do so at once and AVOID INDIGESTION.
White and Brown Bread specially prepared for Invalids visiting Droitwich.

MR EVANS not only manufactured the 'Perfect Loaf' but was the sole agent for Royal Enfield Cycles. What a queer mixture!

A VERY PEACEFUL LOOKING Ombersley Street in the early 1920s.

THIS IS THE IMAGE TO CREATE. A fine picture of George Wythe's shop in the High Street.

THE NEW GENERAL POST OFFICE in Victoria Square pictured around 1908. According to the clock it was taken at about ten seventeen.

W.H. Smith & Son as it was known in 1929. With little change in outward looks it also still offers good, courteous service.

A VERY PROUD MAN, Mr Alexander Smith, Town Crier of Droitwich 1905 – 1921. I hope he was not as noisy as the present one is.

A SUPERB PICTURE of five generations of the Priddey family. The baby is Fiona Esme Priddey, born 18 June 1893.

MR PRICE who lived in Hanbury Terrace cottages near the toll-house with his pony-drawn bath chair.

A VERY SMART TURN OUT by the Droitwich Territorials on Church Parade, March 1910.

JOHN CORBETT, 1817–1901. My favourite picture of this wonderfully kind man.

THE RESULT OF A TERRIBLE FIRE at the storeroom and stable used by Mr W. Everton of High Street, March 1910. It was the property of the Salt Union and was formerly a salt works, afterwards a Sunday school, called the Ark, and was so used for many years until around 1902.

A LINE OF HORSE-DRAWN VEHICLES in 1910 at the top end of Tagwell Road at its junction with the Holloway.

THESE ATHLETIC LOOKING GENTLEMEN are at the starting line for a race to Bromsgrove and back, in aid of the Hospital Saturday and Sunday Fund.

ST ANDREW'S CHURCH situated at the top of the High Street dates mainly from around 1290. Due to subsidence the tower had to be dismantled in 1928 and it now has a rather squat-looking appearance.

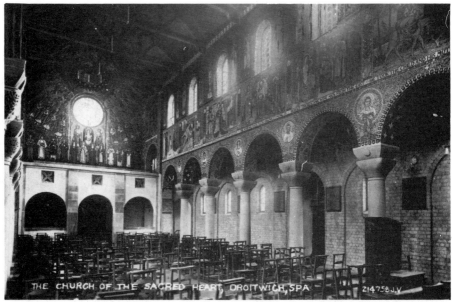

THE CHURCH of the Sacred Heart and St Catherine, a Roman Catholic edifice, which inside has the most marvellous mosaics depicting biblical scenes.

ST NICHOLAS' CHURCH, situated on the west side of Droitwich, where regular services are held for a dedicated congregation.

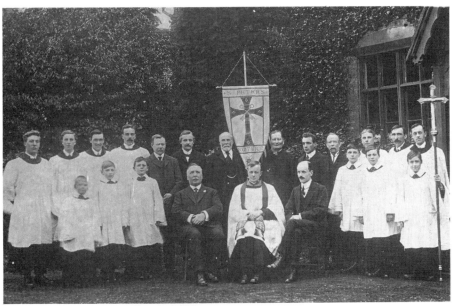

ST PETER'S CHURCH CHOIR, taken in 1915.

THIS LOVELY PICTURE shows some of the residents of St Peter's Walk celebrating a Royal event. Contrary to local opinion, I believe it was to celebrate the coronation of King Edward VII in 1902.

SUNDAY AFTERNOON IN THE PARK on 17 July 1903. Even the band in their thick uniforms look hot.

A NICE QUIET AND SECLUDED PART of the Brine Baths Park.

THE OPEN AIR SWIMMING LIDO is unique in one sense, because the brine, reduced to the density of sea water, is pumped into this spacious pool, 44 yards long and 22 yards wide.

THE ARRIVAL of General Booth of the Salvation Army in 1911.

TOGO, a dog belonging to Mr Harry Laugher used to collect funds for the Red Cross around 1911.

TWO SUPERB PICTURES of the delivery and storage system developed by Everton's Stores. The one has 'horse' power, as does the other.

HERE IS EVERTON'S STORE, situated at the corner of Hanbury Street and Worcester Road in the early 1920s. Just look at that array of fresh produce and the smart young men to serve.

HIGHFIELD HOUSE was acquired by the Birmingham Hospital Saturday and Sunday Fund, who made alterations and considerable additions to turn it into Highfield Hospital. The patients in those days came mainly from the Birmingham area.

41625 Droitwich. St. John's Brine Baths Hospital.

ST JOHN'S HOSPITAL in the Holloway was used by what was then known as the working class. The hospital was dependant on subscriptions, so the patient's length of stay was also dependant on this amount.

303|15 Mens' Sitting Room, St. John's Hospital, Droitwich Spa

St. Andrews Brine Baths, Droitwich

THE ST ANDREW'S BRINE BATHS built by John Corbett in 1882 and extended in 1907 by the trustees, worked miracles for many people, the 'cure' taking about three weeks of treatment.

LADIES' SWIMMING BATH, ST ANDREW'S BRINE BATHS, DROITWICH

MANY ATHLETES used the Brine Baths to tone up before their activities. Here we have a first division team of footballers after their treatment.

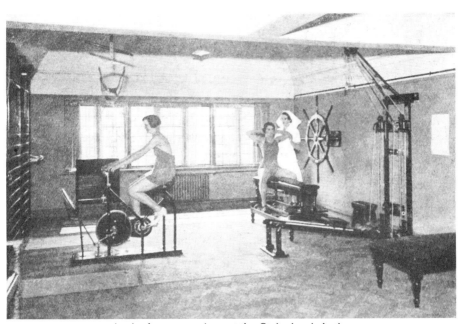

TWO PATIENTS at exercise in the gymnasium at the St Andrew's baths.

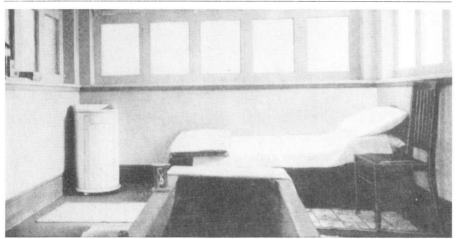

VARIOUS TREATMENTS were available such as the Nauheim bath for heart disorders.

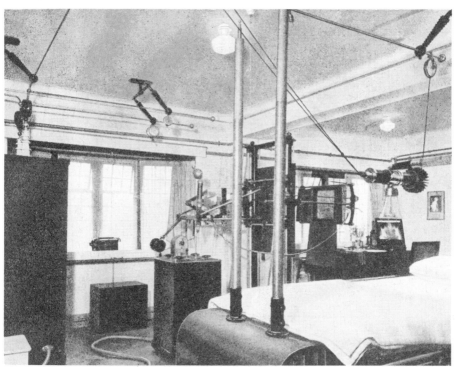

THIS IS the 'complete x-ray apparatus for diagnosis before treatment is specified,' believe it or not.

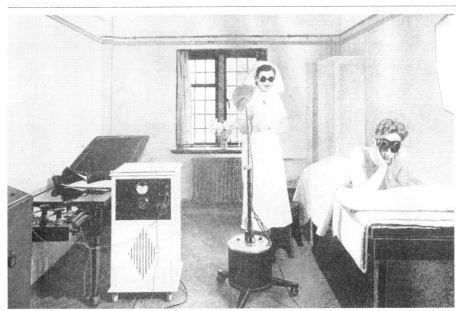

HERE THE POOR PATIENT is in one of the treatment rooms, showing the condenser couch and receiving ultra-violet ray treatment!

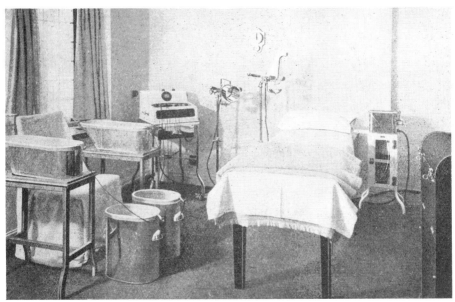

IF THEY GET YOU IN HERE then you will be attacked by high frequency apparatus and tunstone arcs!

A FOOTBALL MATCH procession to collect money for the Saturday and Sunday Hospital fund. March 1910.

THE COMMITTEE OF THE CHARITY SPORTS, who distributed monies collected by various organizations. July 1910.

THE COMPETITORS in a shooting match on Saturday 17 September 1910, between the Veteran Volunteers and the Territorials. The Veterans won the match.

A PRESENTATION to Mr A.J. Bearcroft (centre front row), in some small way to recognise all the work he had put in for the people of Droitwich. The presentation was made in June 1910.

MR A.E. CHAPPELL'S annual spring horse show and sale, held in a field near the GWR Hotel. In this year of 1910, it attracted over one hundred entries.

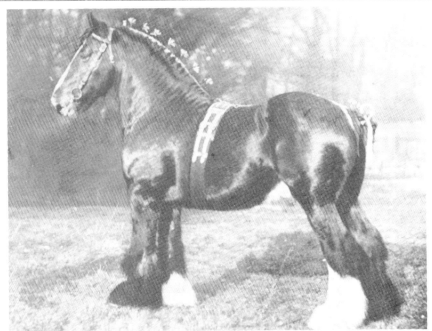

TWO OUTSTANDING BAYS — above: Finstall Ryman standing at over 17 hands and, below: Finstall Regent, at around 16 hands high. Both stallions covered mares in the Droitwich area.

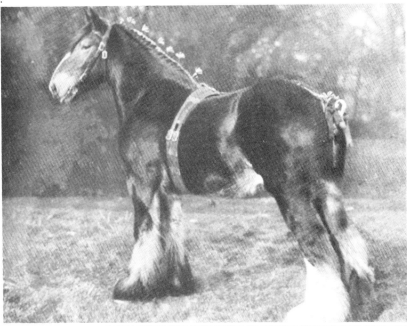

A FINE PICTURE of Dodderhill Church at the top right and the canal leading to the locks and salt works.

A PEACEFUL SCENE at Wheeler's Bridge with a father and daughter out for a Sunday stroll. A houseboat, a popular possession in those days is tied up to the bank.

DODDERHILL CHURCH BELLS
RE-HUNG 1932.

THE HEAVY WEIGHT BELLS from Dodderhill Church prior to their rehanging in 1932.

A POPULAR MEETING SPOT it seems, next to the letter box on Dodderhill Common.

SALT, which had been the making of Droitwich, many years ago, is represented in this volume by only one picture, and that is of James Sparkes, nicknamed 'Jimmy Fake'. There were many types of nickname used for local people years ago, but all had some sort of meaning. Whether it was to their advantage or not is very uncertain.

Saltworker filling tub · Droitwich

A MODEL of a Roman vase found at Chester, and the Droitwich heraldic emblem put on the side by Goss, the most famous of all fine china makers.

THE DEMOLITION of one of the old salt works by men such as Reuben Sparkes, Thomas Slater, Geo Harry Bourne, Albert Crowther, Bert Constable, Samuel Crowther and William Bourne. Note Dodderhill church in the background.

THE OLD SMITHY at Tower Hill. For many years it was what its name implies, and has been used for a variety of jobs since then, even in the early sixties as a safe factory.

TWO FINE PICTURES of nurses and servicemen convalescing at the Oaklands during the First World War.

THE HON. J.C. LYTTLETON and some of his supporters outside his committee rooms, January 1910.

THE HON. J.C. LYTTELTON and some more of his supporters during election fever at Droitwich, 29 January 1910.

SCENES AT DROITWICH for the mid-Worcestershire elections, when Mr C. Harmsworth (Radical) stood against Mr J.C. Lyttelton, (Unionist). Some ugly moments developed when it was clear that Mr Lyttelton would win.

THE DECLARATION OF THE POLL, when Mr Lyttelton defeated Mr Harmsworth by 105 votes. Polling day being 29 January 1910.

THE RIOT ACT having been read during the election, a number of men stood accused of 'Riotous Behaviour', amongst them were Messrs: Sankey, Sparkes, Pittaway, Priddey, Evans, Harrison, Green and Bateman.

OUTSIDE THE CROOKED HOUSE or Wagon & Horses pub in the High Street with the locals celebrating the coronation of King Edward VII in 1902.

TWO ELDERLY INMATES of the Coventry Charity Almshouses enjoying a chat in the sun.

MR S. BENNETT of Hadzor won the first prize in the Droitwich Farmers Club competition for Mangolds, with a little help from Hadfield's 'Special Mangold Manure,' of course.

WHAT DO YOU THINK OF ME in this photo taken at Droitwich? So asks the writer of this card. Can anyone enlighten me as to what it is all about? The nurses should be a clue, but the men with their buttonholes?

HERE IS ANOTHER ONE. It can be seen that the cart is from Mr F. Somer, butcher, Droitwich, but why a distribution of meat for the employees of the Salt Union and where?

DROITWICH SEEMS TO HAVE, OR HAVE HAD, MORE NICKNAMES PER HEAD OF POPULATION THAN ANY OTHER PLACE THAT I KNOW OF. IT IS AMAZING WHAT YOU FIND IF YOU DIG DEEP ENOUGH. TRY THESE:

Tit Bullock
Darkie Bourne
Salty Bourne
Jimmy Old Hen Bourne
Rabbit Bourne
Tich Bayliss
Barber Bourne
Boxer Bourne
Dodger Bourne
Dandy Bourne
Gory Bourne
Banner Bourne
Swank Bourne
Whiskers Bateman
Sandy Crowther
Toodles Colley
Spare Me Cottrill
Wavy Cottrill
Yankee Davis
Rackam Duggan
Skydrift Evans
Cuggie Elvins
Lamp Lighter Elvins
Rock Everton
Farmer Fox
Tommy Frail
Cabbage Goddard

Fantail Harris
Nin Harris
Tank Harris
Stringer Harris
Cloggy Harrison
Buffer Harrison
Tea Harrison
Twenty Pint Jack
Shorty Knight
Dubber Maycroft
Fatty Nicklin
Shuck Noggy
Preezer Price
Darkus Priddy
George Count Priddy
Cuckoo Pittaway
China Prosser
Bodger Pugh
Filly Smith
Wat Sankey
Jimmy Fake Sparkes
Skinner Sparkes
Larker Sparkes
Monkey Sparkes
Taffy Tarpy
Bab Ward
Tar Tivy

ACKNOWLEDGEMENTS

How does one say thank you to all the kind people who have lent or given me their postcards and pictures for inclusion in this book? The only way here is to put their names in print and to say how much we appreciate their generosity and support. The names are in no particular order. They are just as I scribbled them down in my dog-eared notebook. As there is no mixed bathing allowed I have separated the ladies from the men!

Messrs:- W. Wilcox ● F. Platts ● J. Hoskins ● C. Bull ● W.H. Smith Ltd.
C. Jennings ● Heritage Centre ● P. Baldwin ● T. McCarthy ● A. Wilson
F. Smith ● T. Fincher ● A. Hemsley ● G. Sawyer

Mesdames:-A. Rowley ● E. Fellows ● J. Thomas ● W. Hayward
J. Butterworth ● D. Marshall ● N. Smith ● C. Bull ● E. Cooper ● V. Day
M. Harris ● R. Preece ● M. Reeves ● E. Salisbury.